1000 SIGHT WORDS THE ULTIMATE VOCABULARY BOOK

PICTURE DICTIONARY WITH SENTENCE

English - Serbian

action

акције

Action!

actually

заправо

I actually like strawberry.

adjective

придев

Tell me an adjective to describe this.

afraid

бојим се

What are you afraid of?

agreed

договорили

They agreed on music.

ahead

напред

Who was ahead in the race?

allow

допустити

Did the teacher allow him to go play?

apple

јабука

Eat an apple.

arrived

стигао

My plane arrived on time.

born

рођен

Where were you born?

bought

купљено

She bought new clothes.

British

британци

Who is the British monarch?

capital

главни град

The capital is in Washington DC.

chance

шанса

Dice is a game of chance.

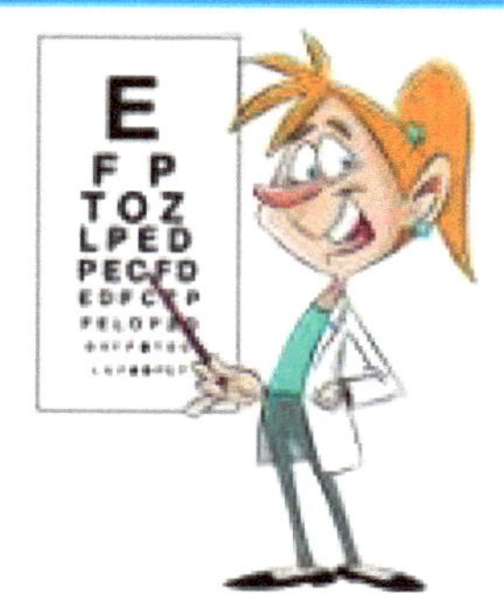

chart

графикон

What does your medical chart say?

church

црква

Did you go to church?

column

колона

Did you read the newspaper column?

company

компанија

What company do you work for?

conditions

услови

What are the weather conditions.

corn

кукуруз

Do you like corn?

cotton

памук

A q-tip is made of cotton.

cows

крава

How many cows does he have?

create

креирај

What art did you create?

dead

мртав

The bug is dead.

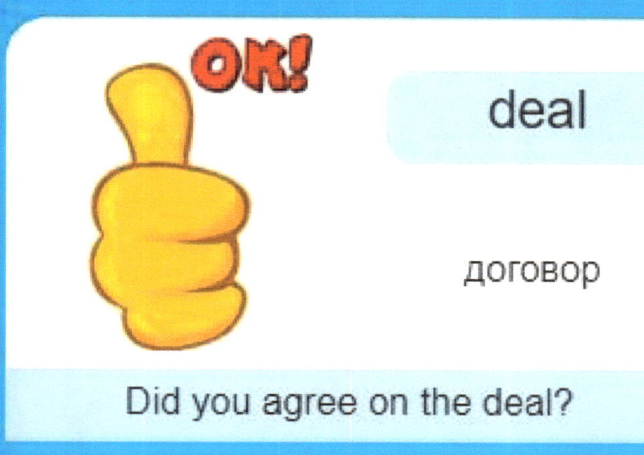

deal

договор

Did you agree on the deal?

death

смрт

The grim reaper is death.

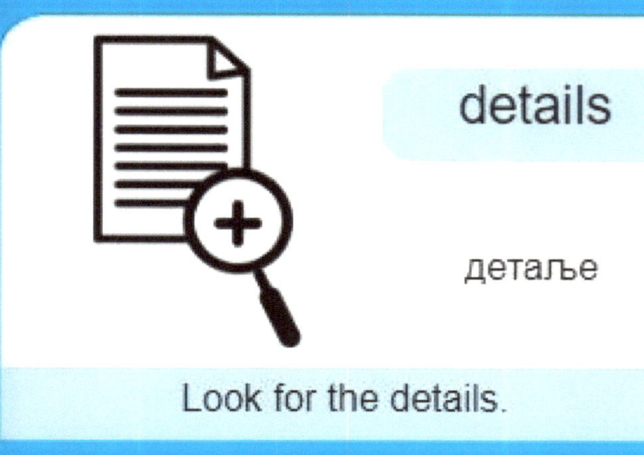

details

детаље

Look for the details.

determine

одредити

Did you determine where to go eat?

difficult

тешко

I found this difficult.

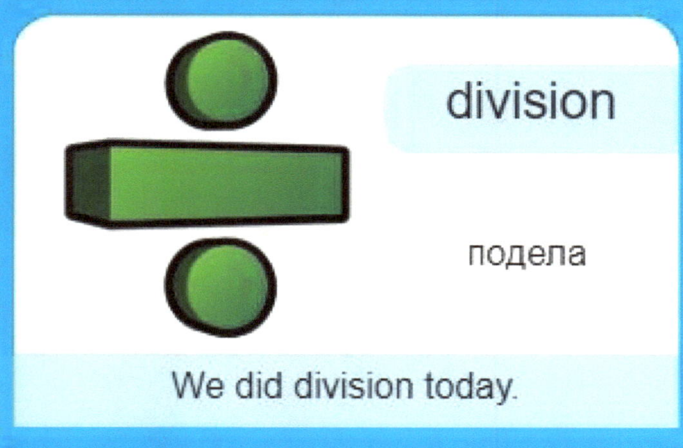

division

подела

We did division today.

doesn't

не

Doesn't it sound beautiful?

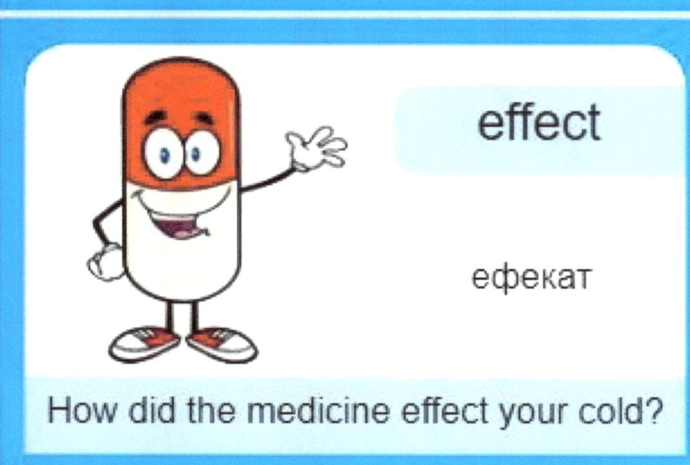

effect

ефекат

How did the medicine effect your cold?

entire

цео

The entire family was in the picture.

especially

посебно

She especially liked writing.

evening

вече

The ceremony was this evening.

experience

искуство

She has a lot of experience.

factories

фабрике

There are a lot of factories there.

fair

забавни парк

Let's go to the fair.

fear

бојати се

I have a huge fear of clowns.

fig

смокве

I ate a fig.

forward

напред

Spring forward the clocks.

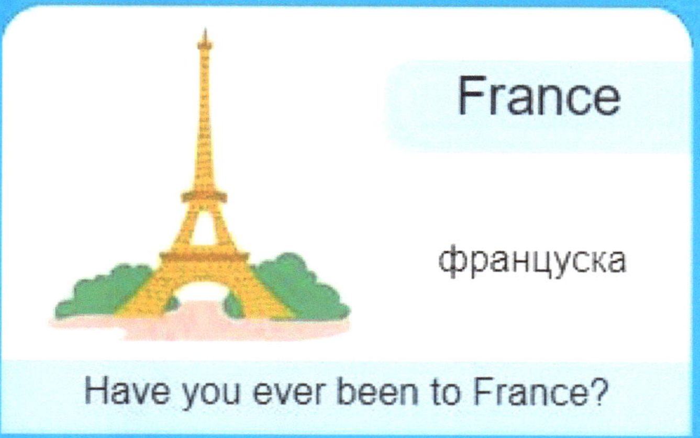

France

француска

Have you ever been to France?

fresh

свеж

All the fruit is fresh.

Greek

грчки

Have you ever had Greek food?

gun

пушке

We played with a water gun.

hoe

мотика

Use a hoe in the garden.

huge

огроман

Those trees are huge!

isn't

није

Isn't it nice to hang out with friends?

led

вођа

The dog led her.

level

ниво

Use the level to hang the picture.

located

налази се

Where is the store located?

march

парада

Are you going to march with the band?

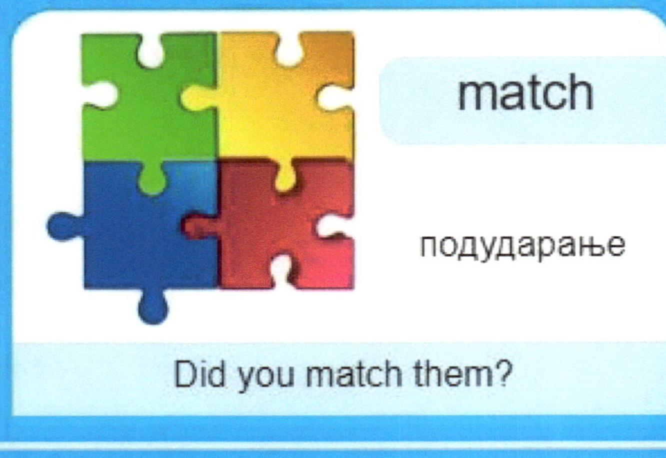

match

подударање

Did you match them?

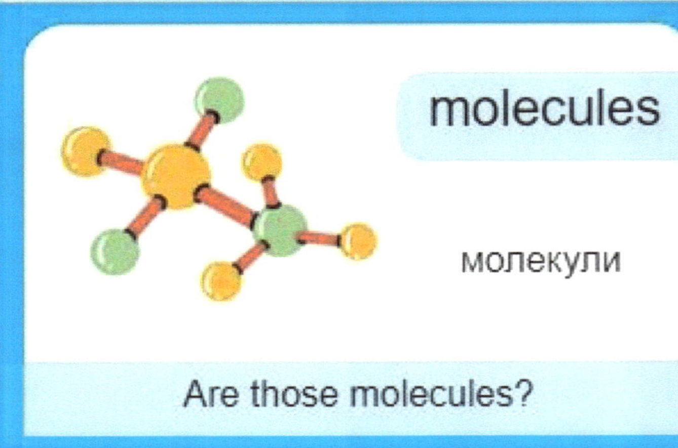

molecules

молекули

Are those molecules?

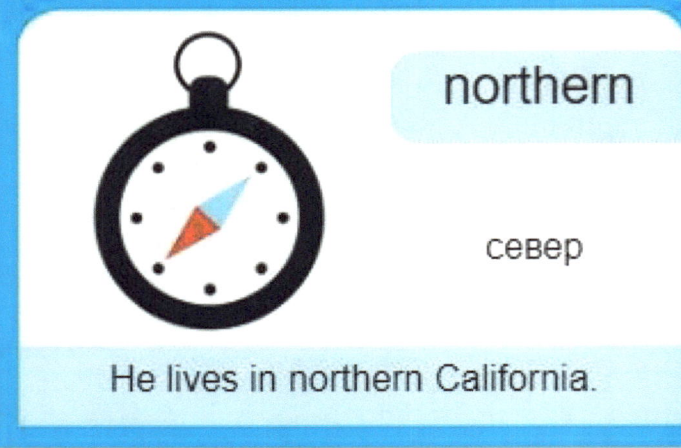

northern

север

He lives in northern California.

nose

нос

My nose is running.

office

канцеларија

Do you need any office supplies?

oxygen

кисеоник

What is the symbol for oxygen?

plural

множина

What is the plural of a mouse?

prepared

припремити

She prepared for the exam.

pretty

прилично

Pretty in pink.

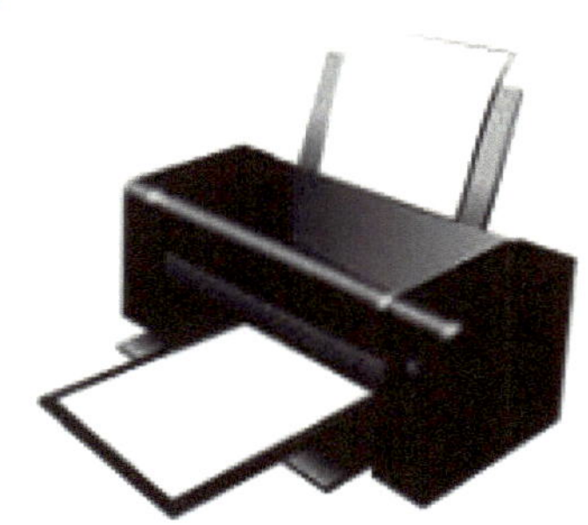

printed

штампано

She printed out the forms.

radio

радио

Let's listen to the radio.

repeated

понављање

They repeated the exercises daily.

rope

конопац

Do you have any rope?

rose

ружа

Thank you for the rose.

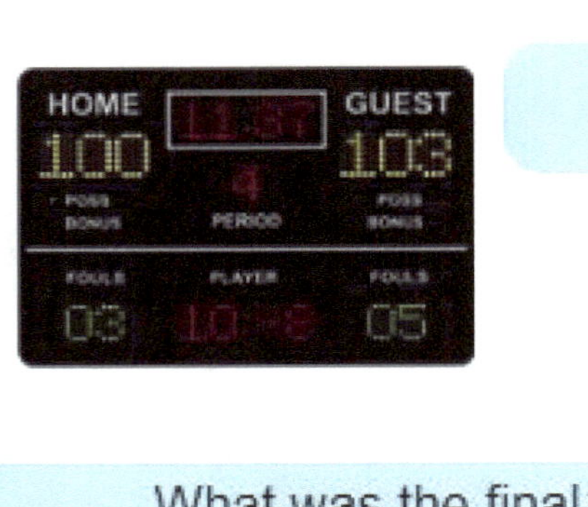

score

резултат

What was the final score?

seat

седиште

The girls took a seat in the sand.

settled

насељавали

The case was settled.

shoes

ципеле

Put your shoes on.

shop

продавнице

I'm need to go shop for groceries.

similar

слично

The halves are similar.

sir

господине

Yes, sir!

sister

сестра

Is she your sister?

smell

мирис

I love the smell of cookies!

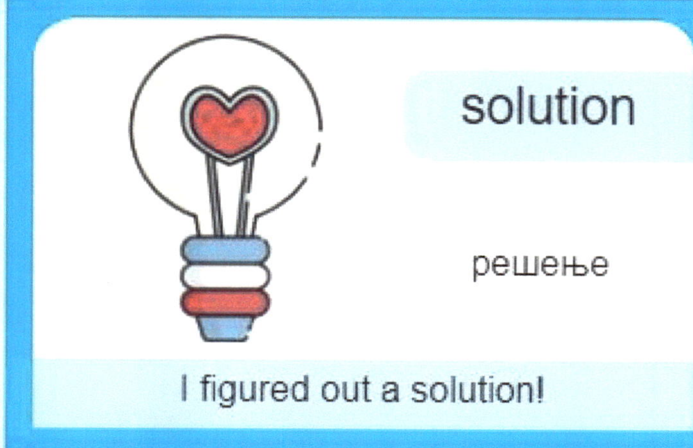

solution

решење

I figured out a solution!

southern

југ

She's a southern belle.

steel

челика

The new building used steel.

stretched

испружен

We stretched before the workout.

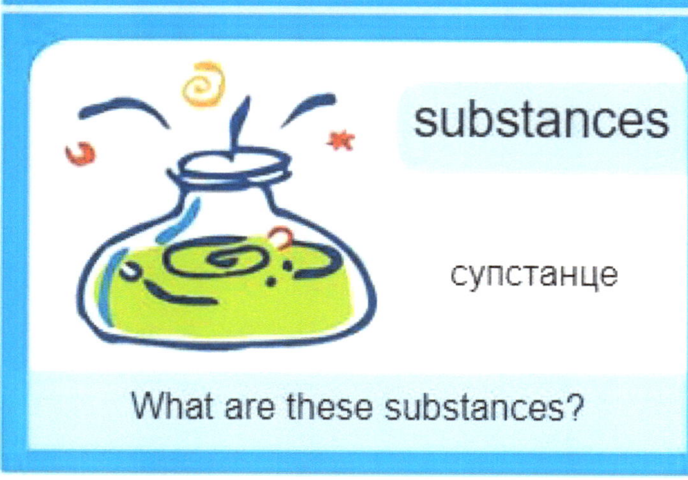

substances

супстанце

What are these substances?

suffix

суфикс

What is the suffix of the word?

sugar

шећер

Sugar cube for your tea?

tools

алате

May I borrow your tools?

total

укупно

What's the total?

track

трацк

The runners got on the track.

triangle

троугао

How many sides does a triangle have?

truck

камион

Is thaty our truck?

underline

<u>underline</u>

подвући

Underline the word.

various

разне

I watch various shows.

view

поглед

That is a beautiful view!

Washington

васхингтон

She is from Washington.

we'll

воља

We'll finish buying our groceries.

western

западни

It's western wear day.

win

победити

Did you win?

woman

жена

The woman was on her way to work.

workers

радник

The workers were busy.

wouldn't

не

Wouldn't you like to go shopping?

wrong

погрешно

Did I get it wrong?

yellow

жута

A banana is yellow.

after

после

You may have dessert after dinner.

again

опет

May we go on the ride again?

air

ваздух

The air was cold.

also

такође

I also like baseball.

America

америка

Columbus sailed to America.

animal

животиња

My favorite animal is a lion.

another

други

Have another cookie.

answer

одговор

Raise your hand to answer.

any

било који

Do you have any crayons?

around

око

Let's travel around the world.

ask

питати

It's good to ask questions.

away

далеко

Throw your trash away.

back

назад

We went back to school.

because

jep

I went to bed because I was tired.

before

пре него што

Sharpen your pencil before the test.

big

велика

The elephant is a big animal.

boy

дечко

The boy played a basketball.

came

дошао

He came to class.

change

промена

I save my change.

different

различит

They use different balls.

does

урадите

Does he ride the bus?

end

крај

She watched to the end.

even

чак

They learned about even numbers.

follow

пратити

Follow the teacher.

form

форма

Complete the form.

found

нашао

We found a puppy.

give

дај

I like to give gifts.

good

добро

The hamburger was good.

great

велики

Great job!

hand
рука
Please hand in your work.

help
помоћ
You should help others.

here
овде
Do you sit here?

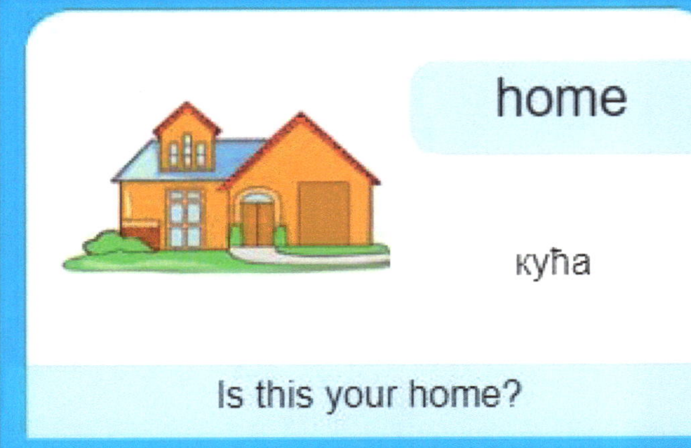

home
кућа
Is this your home?

house
куца
The doll house was pink.

just
само
The train just left.

kind
будите љубазни
Be kind to each other.

know
знам
I don't know.

land

фарма

They bought some land.

large

велика

A bear is large.

learn

научите

It's fun to learn science.

letter

писмо

He mailed a letter.

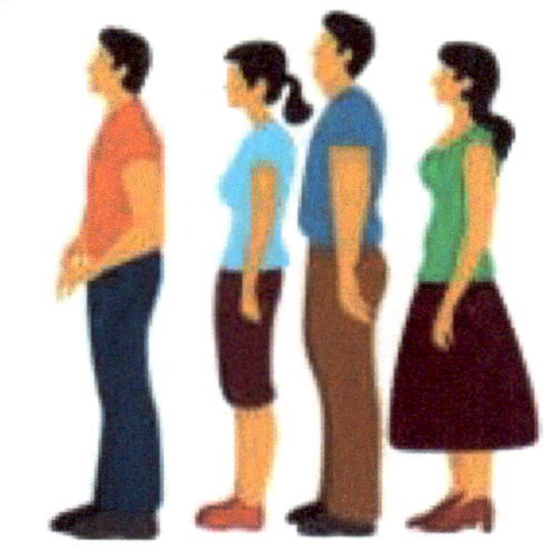

line

линије

Please form a line.

little

мало

He has a little sister.

live

уживо

You live in the city.

man

човек

The man drove.

me

ja

Come with me to the park.

means

значи

She got her by means of a taxi.

men

мушкарци

The men played football.

most

већина

Most students like to help.

mother

мајке

He loves his mother.

move

потез

His family decided to move.

much

много

How much is the camera?

must

мора

You must raise your hand.

name

име

What is his name?

need

желим

Do you need to sleep?

new

нова

We have a new teacher.

off

ван

The rocket blasted off.

old

стари

Those are old toys.

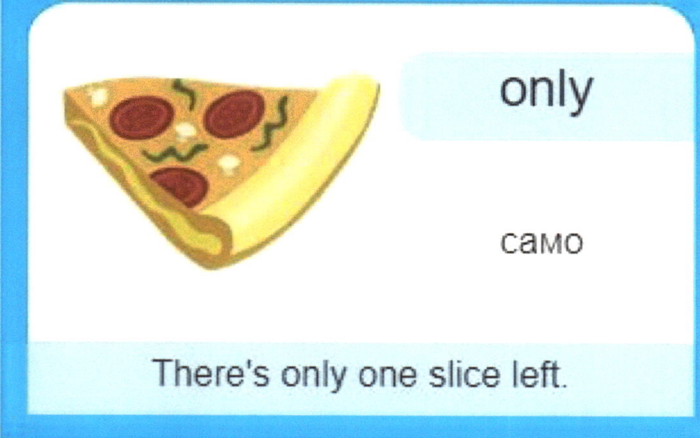

only

само

There's only one slice left.

our

наше

She was our teacher.

over

преко

He jumped over it.

page

страна

Please turn the page.

picture

слика

They took their picture.

place

место

This is my favorite place.

play

игра

Let's play together!

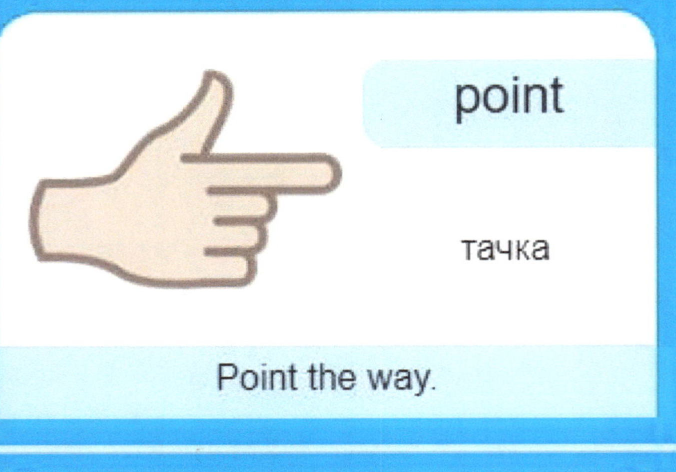

point

тачка

Point the way.

put

ставити

Please put the supplies away.

read

читати

Do you like to read?

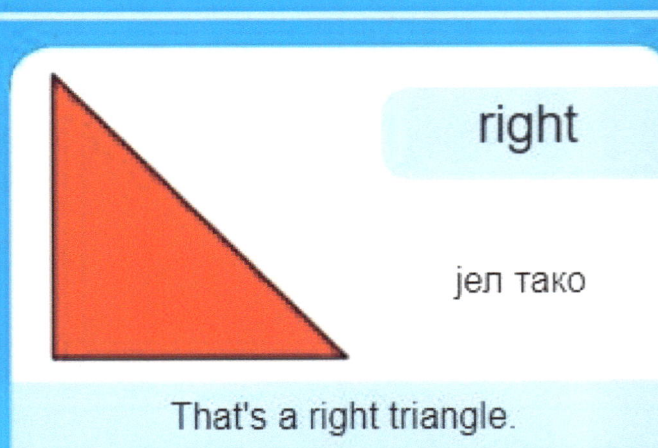

right

јел тако

That's a right triangle.

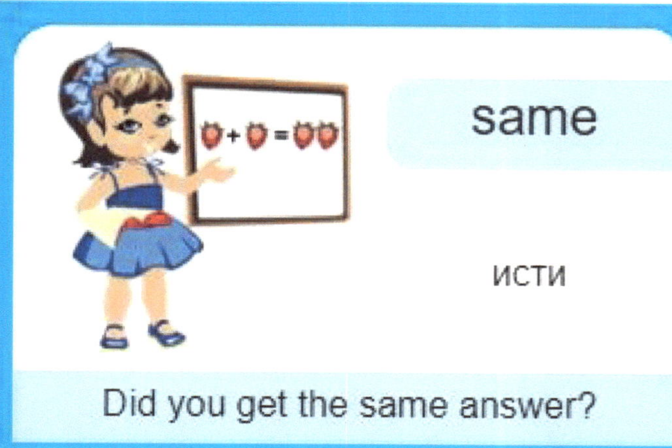

same

исти

Did you get the same answer?

say

реците

What did you say?

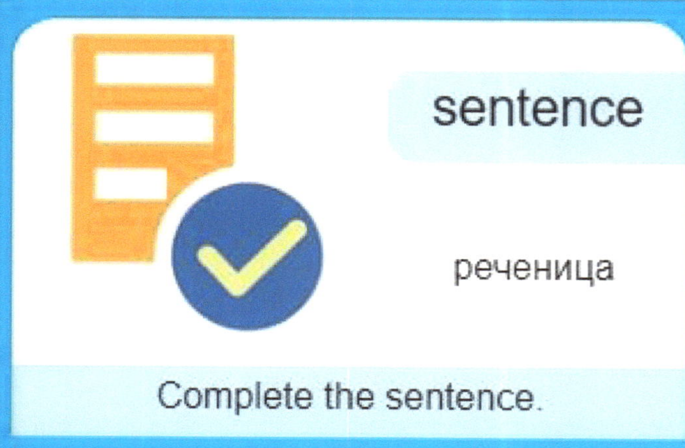

sentence

реченица

Complete the sentence.

set

комплет

Please set the table.

should

требало би

We should exercise.

show

прикажи

Show your work.

small

мала

The ladybug is small.

sound

звук

A bee makes a buzzing sound.

spell

чаролија

Please spell the word.

still

још увек

I still want ice skates.

study

студија

It's time to study.

such

такве

He is such a good dog.

take

узми

Please take your seat.

tell

реци

She wanted to tell a secret.

things

ствари

She washed a lot of things.

think

мисли

Think about it.

three

три

It's the number three.

through

кроз

He was through with the race.

too

такође

Do you like chocolate too?

try

покушати

Try again, please.

turn

ред

Turn in your homework.

us

нас

She taught us.

very

врло

He is a very good singer.

want

желим

I want to ride my bike.

well

добро

You did well.

went

отишао

We went to recess.

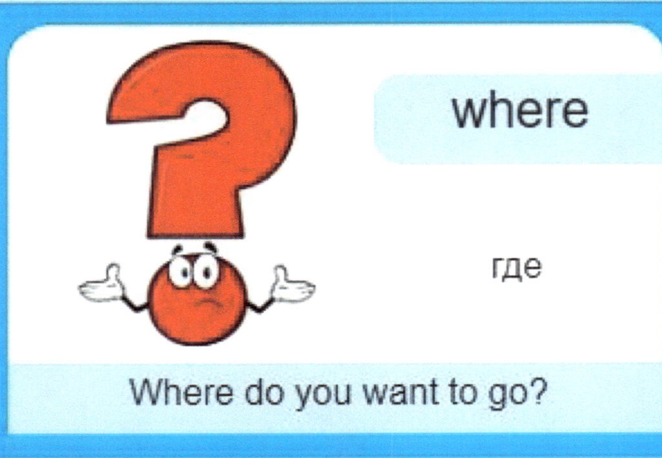

where

где

Where do you want to go?

why

зашто

She asked why?

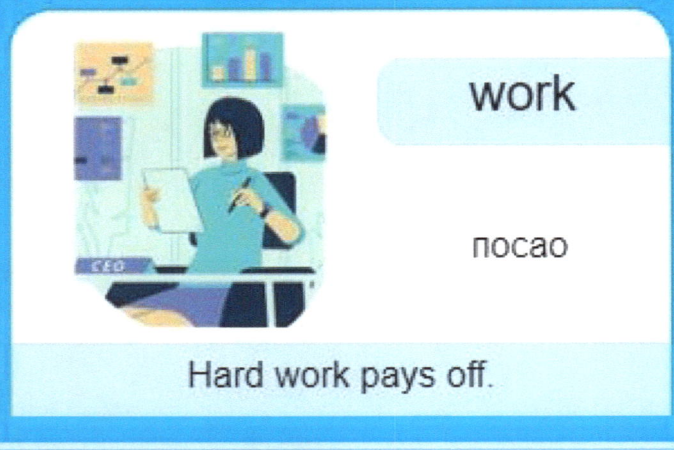

work

посао

Hard work pays off.

world

свет

I want to travel the world.

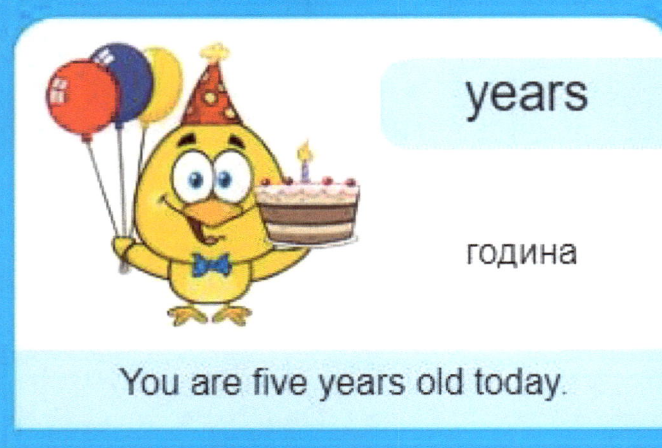

years

година

You are five years old today.

above

горе

The sky was above them.

add

додати

If you add one plus two, you get three.

almost

скоро

It's almost lunch time.

along

заједно

We get along.

always

увек

She always brushes her teeth.

began

почело

The baby began to cry.

begin

започети

You may begin your exam.

being

биће

She is being shy.

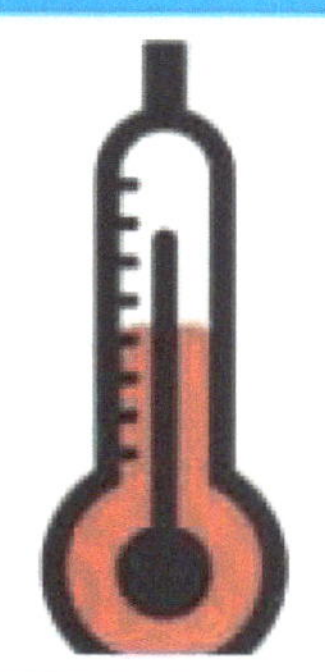

below

испод

It's below thirty degrees.

between

између

Two is between one and three.

book

књига

I'm reading this book.

both

и једно и друго

They both worked on math.

car

ауто

He bought a new car.

carry

носити

She had a bag to carry her groceries.

children

деца

Four children sang.

city

град

He worked in the city.

close

близу

Please close the door.

country

земљу

Do you live in the country?

cut

исећи

You use scissors to cut.

don't

не

Don't forget!

earth

земља

Our planet is Earth.

eat

јести

I eat bananas.

enough

довољно

Did you eat enough pancakes?

every

сваки

I shower every day.

example

пример

This is an example of a bird.

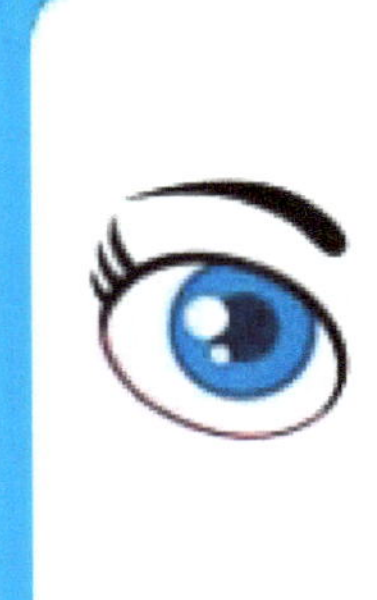

eyes

очи

What color are her eyes?

face

лице

They were at the face painting booth.

family

породица

How big is your family?

far

далеко

How far is it?

father

отац

Her father walked her to school.

feet

стопала

Put socks on your feet.

few

неколико

She wanted a few more minutes.

food

храна

They made a lot of food.

four

четири

There were four of them.

girl

девојка

The girl wore pink shoes.

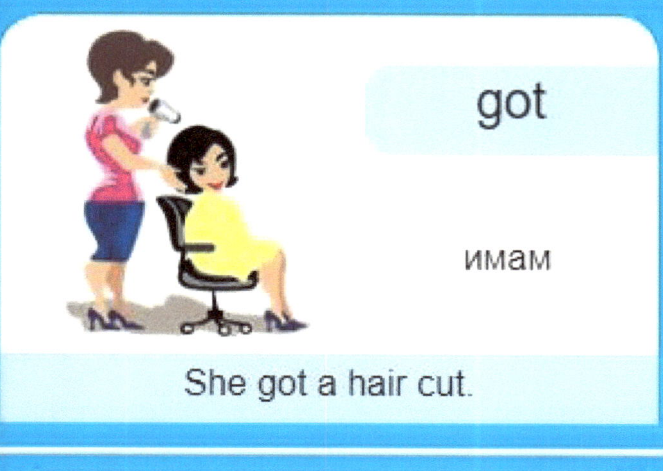

got

имам

She got a hair cut.

group

група

They were working in a group.

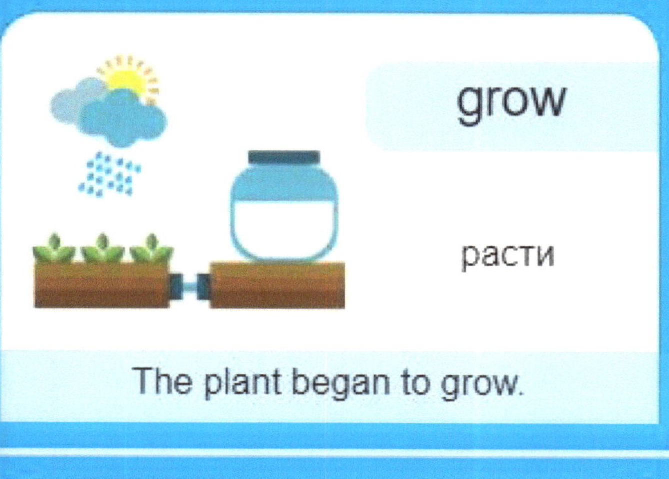

grow

расти

The plant began to grow.

hard

тешко

He wore a hard hat.

head

глава

He wore a cap on his head.

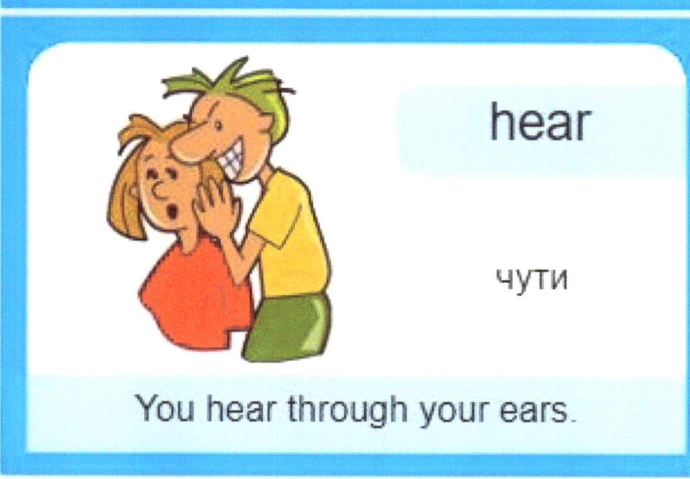

hear

чути

You hear through your ears.

high

високо

She wore high heels.

idea

идеја

I have an idea!

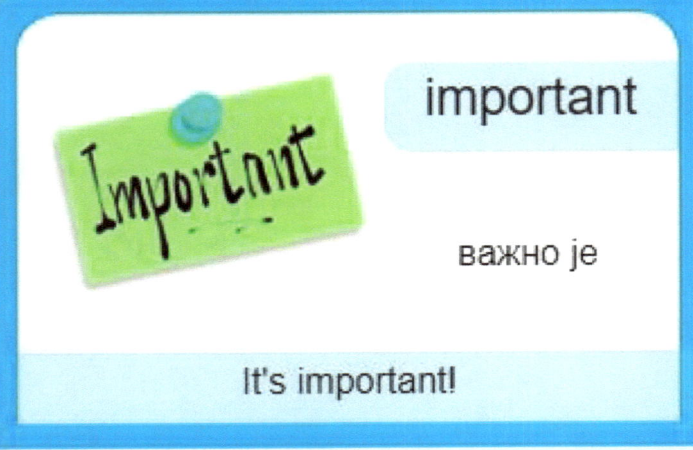

important

важно је

It's important!

Indian

индијанац

It's an Indian elephant.

it's

је

It's a tiger cub.

keep

задржати

Can you keep a secret?

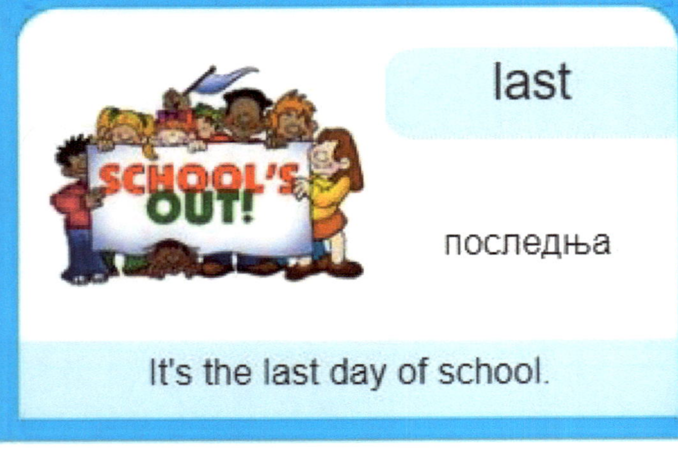

last

последња

It's the last day of school.

late

касно

You're late.

leave

отићи

He packed to leave.

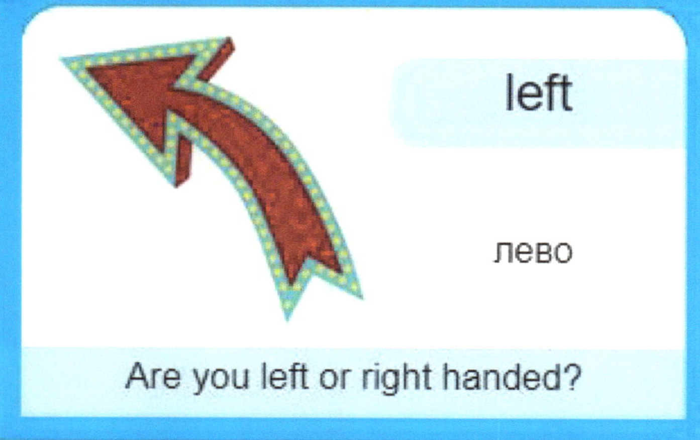

left

лево

Are you left or right handed?

let

дозволити

Will you let me go fishing?

life

живот

Life is about friends and family.

light

светло

The light turned yellow.

list

листа

Here's my to-do list

might

можда

It might rain today.

mile

миљу

It's a mile from here.

miss

господица

You may correct any you miss.

mountains

планина

There are alot of mountains here.

near

близу

We are near the beach.

never

никад

I've never broken my leg.

next

следећи

Take the next step.

night

ноћ

You can see the stars at night.

often

често

How often do you watch tv?

once

једном

Once upon a time…

The door is open.

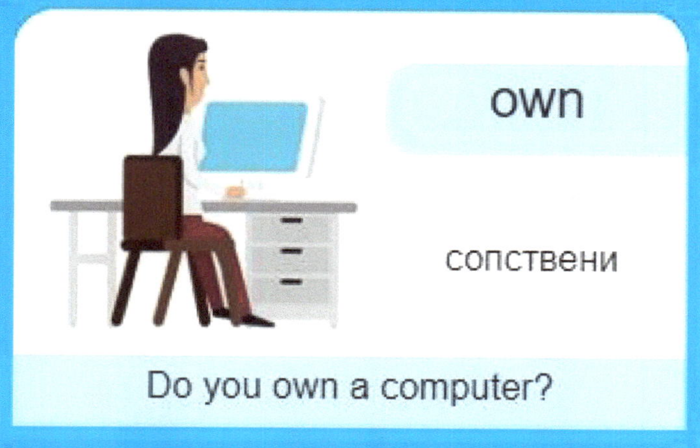

Do you own a computer?

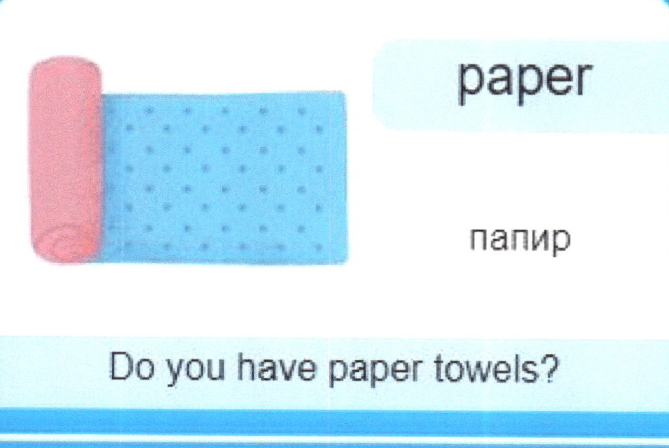

Do you have paper towels?

I will water the plant.

Her real name is Sally.

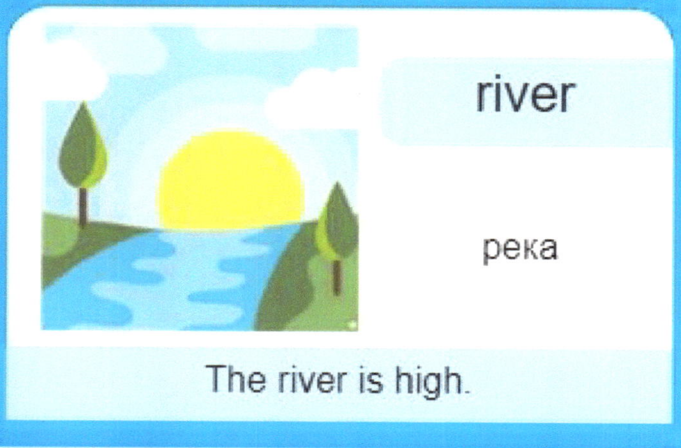

The river is high.

He likes to run with his dog.

We saw a UFO.

school

школа

Do you like school?

sea

море

The ship is at sea.

second

друго

She won second place.

seem

изгледа

You seem busy.

side

страна

Each side of a square is the same.

something

нешто

Did you hear something?

sometimes

понекад

Sometimes we watch tv.

song

сонг

We will sing a song.

soon

ускоро

Dinner will be ready soon.

start

почетак

Start writing.

state

стање

Which state do you live in?

stop

зауставити

Do you see the stop sign?

story

прича

What's the story about?

talk

причај

Let's talk.

those

оне

Those are great cookies!

thought

мисао

I thought the novel was good.

together

зајeдно

They went shopping together.

took

узми

He took the last piece.

tree

дрво

Did you decorate the tree?

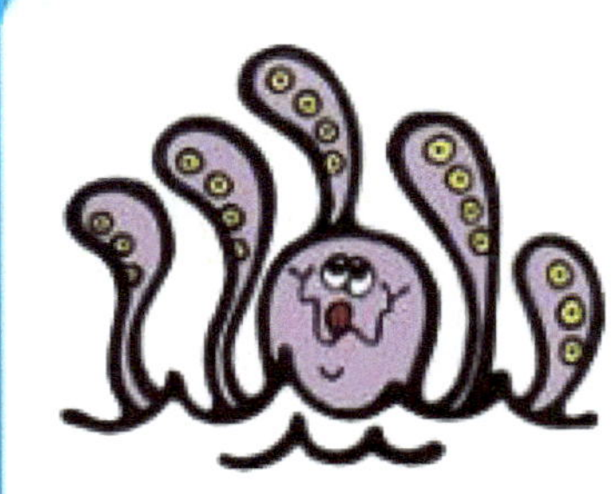

under

испод

It lives under the sea.

until

све док

I work until 5 o'clock.

walk

ходати

We went for a walk.

watch

ручни сат

Do you wear a watch?

while

док

We had fun while skiing.

white

бео

They drew on the white board.

without

без

I can't go without my backpack.

young

млад

Her kids are young.

across

широм

It's across the street.

against

против

It's against the rules.

area

област

There are no wild animals in this area.

become

постаните

It will become a butterfly.

best

најбоље

Do your best!

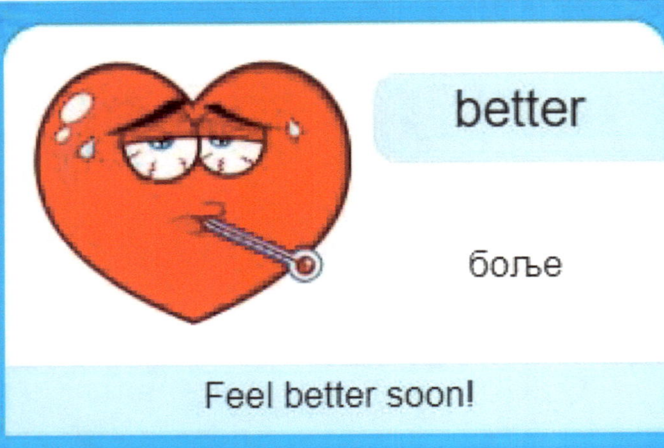

better

боље

Feel better soon!

birds

птица

There's a lot of birds.

black

црн

He has a black cat.

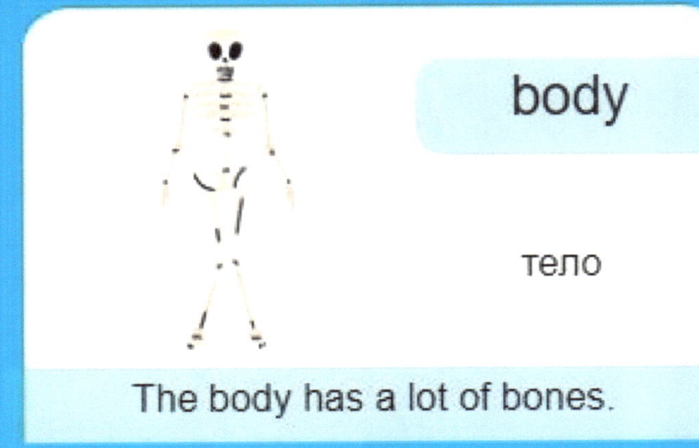

body

тело

The body has a lot of bones.

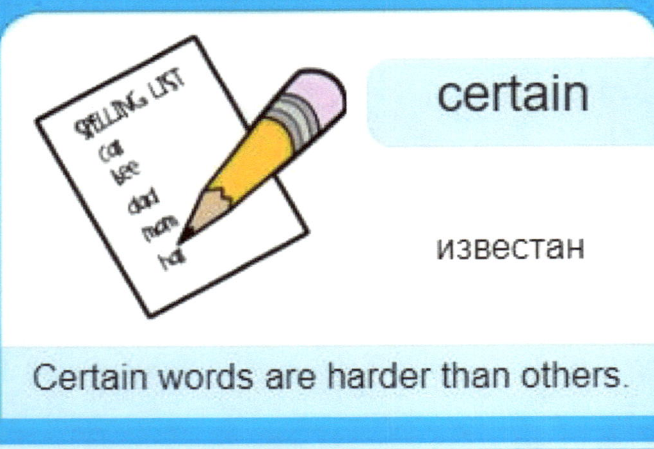

certain

известан

Certain words are harder than others.

cold

хладно

It's cold outside.

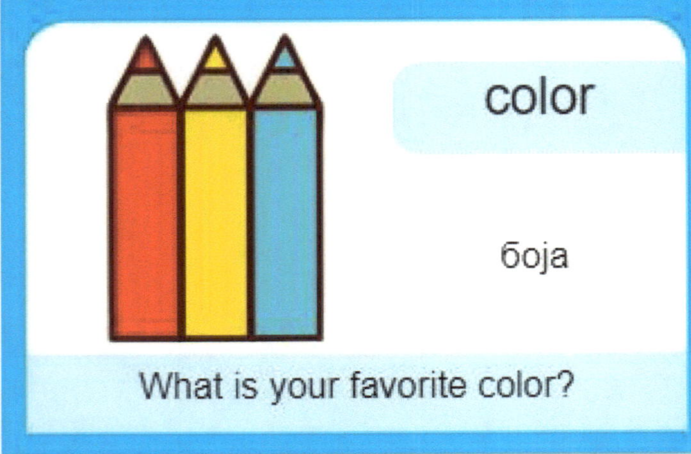

color

боја

What is your favorite color?

complete

комплетан

Did you complete your workout?

www.ingramcontent.com/pod-product-compliance
Lightning Source LLC
Chambersburg PA
CBHW042007110726
48006CB00004B/1001